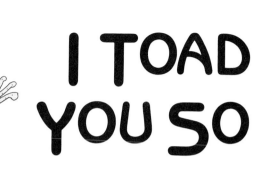

# I TOAD YOU SO

*Riddles about Frogs and Toads*

by Rick and Ann Walton

pictures by Susan Slattery Burke

**L** Lerner Publications Company · Minneapolis

*To Patrick, who makes us hoppy*   —R.W. & A.W.

*To my wonderful daughter, Shea, for her incredible
inspiration in this first year of her life*   —S.S.B.

This edition of this book is available in two bindings:
Library binding by Lerner Publications Company
Soft cover by First Avenue Editions
241 First Avenue North
Minneapolis, Minnesota 55401

Library of Congress Cataloging-in-Publication Data

Walton, Rick.
   I toad you so: riddles about frogs and toads/by Rick and Ann
Walton; pictures by Susan Slattery Burke.

      p.      cm.—(You must be joking)
   Summary: A collection of riddles about frogs and toads, including
"What does a frog do if he gets sick? He gets a hoperation."
   ISBN 0-8225-2331-0 (lib. bdg.)
   ISBN 0-8225-9590-7 (pbk.)
   1. Riddles, Juvenile. 2. Frogs—Juvenile humor. 3. Toads—
Juvenile humor. [1. Frogs—Wit and humor. 2. Toads—Wit and
humor. 3. Riddles.] I. Walton, Ann, 1963-      . II. Burke, Susan
Slattery, ill. III. Title. IV. Series.
PN6371.5.W355   1991         818'.5402—dc20         90-49275
                                                    CIP
Manufactured in the United States of America      AC

1  2  3  4  5  6  7  8  9  10  00  99  98  97  96  95  94  93  92  91

**Q:** What should you say to a one-year-old frog?

**A:** "Hoppy Birthday!"

**Q**: What goes "hop, hop, hop, POP!"?
**A**: A frog chewing bubble gum.

**Q**: Why are frogs always smiling?
**A**: Because they're hoppy.

**Q**: What goes "hop, hop, hop, tumble, tumble, tumble"?
**A**: A clumsy frog trying to hop down stairs.

**Q:** How do frogs play Ping-Pong?
**A:** With a lily paddle.

**Q:** What game do frogs play?
**A:** Hopscotch.

**Q:** What do frogs play when they're done with hopscotch?
**A:** Toadlywinks.

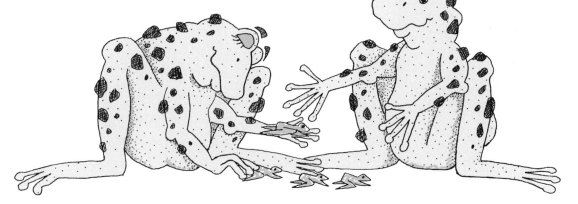

Q: What do frogs play on quiet afternoons?
A: Croakquet.

**Q**: What do frogs like to eat at baseball games?

**A**: Hop dogs.

**Q**: What do frogs like to drink at baseball games?

**A**: Pop flies.

**Q**: If you go fishing for frogs, what should you use?

**A**: A toadpole.

**Q**: What do you call it when a lake is filled with baby frogs?

**A**: Tadpollution.

**Q:** What game do toads play with a rope?

**A:** Tug-of-wart.

**Q**: What track-and-field event do frogs excel at?
**A**: The tadpole vault.

**Q**: How can you tell how high a frog jumps?
**A**: Measure her altitoad.

**Q**: When frogs fly airplanes, where do they like to sit?
**A**: In the croakpit.

**Q**: What should you do if your frog breaks down?
**A**: Call a toad truck.

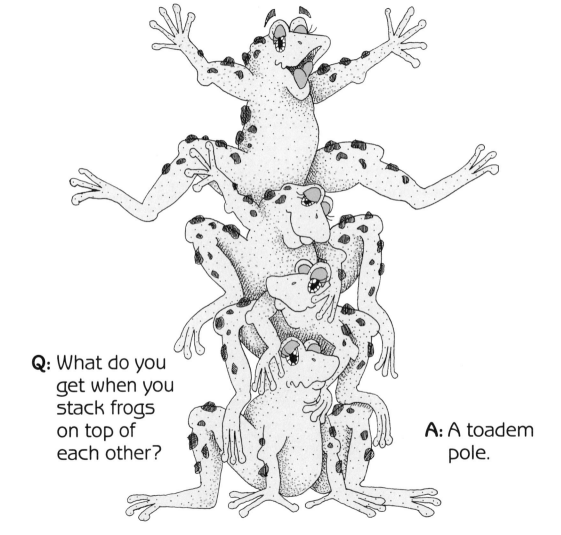

**Q:** What do you get when you stack frogs on top of each other?

**A:** A toadem pole.

**Smart Frog:** What's the quickest way to make one piece of paper into two pieces?

**Smarter Frog:** Rippit.

**Q:** How fast can a frog stick out his tongue?

**A:** In the twinkling of a fly.

**Q:** Why don't sad frogs jump?

**A:** Because they're unhoppy.

**Smart Frog:** What should you do if you find a magic lamp?

**Smarter Frog:** Rubbit.

**Q:** What do you get when you cross a bull with a frog?

**A:** A horned toad.

**Q:** What do you get when you cross a frog with a pig?

**A:** A warthog.

**Smart Frog:** What has four feet, a furry tail, and hops?

**Smarter Frog:** Rabbit.

**Q:** What's green, weighs 4,000 pounds, and likes to jump on people?

**A:** A hoppopotamus.

**Q:** Where should you go if your frog needs glasses?

**A:** The hoptometrist.

**Q:** Why do people like to hire frogs to work for them?

**A:** Because when a frog has a job to do, she hops to it.

**Q:** How do frogs lift heavy objects?

**A:** They use pulleywogs.

**Q:** Who arrests speeding frogs?

**A:** The hop cop and the tadpolice.

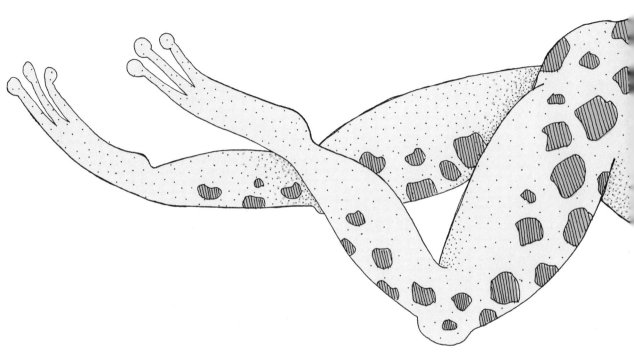

**Q:** What's eight feet long, has sharp
teeth, and hops through the swamp?

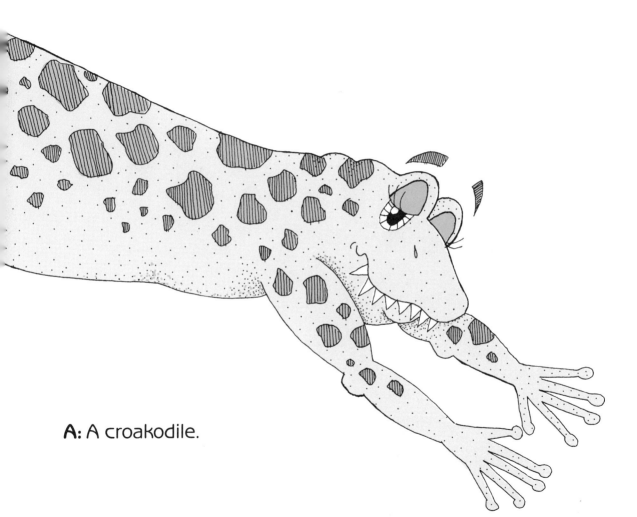

**A:** A croakodile.

**Q:** What do you get when you plant a frog?

**A:** A cr-oak tree.

**Q:** What do you get when you cut down the cr-oak tree?

**A:** A frog log.

**Q:** What can you build with frog logs?

**A:** Greenhouses.

**Q:** What's the nicest thing you can say to a frog?

**A:** Go jump in a lake.

**Q:** What flowers do frogs grow in their gardens?

**A:** Croakcuses and tuleaps.

**Q:** What do frogs wear in the rain?

**A:** Pondchos.

**Q:** What do you get when you cross a frog with a calendar?

**A:** A leap year.

**Q:** What do frogs like to drink in the winter?

**A:** Hot croakoa.

**Q**: What would you have if the air were full of frogs?

**A**: Frog smog.

**Q**: How do you keep from crashing into frogs in the dark?

**A**: Blow your froghorn.

**Q**: What kind of weather do witches like?

**A**: When it's raining cats and frogs.

**Q**: How do you clean a dirty frog?

**A**: With a hop mop.

**Q:** Who should you call if you need to get in touch with a frog?

**A:** The hoperator.

**Q:** How do you address a letter to a frog?

**A:** With the zip toad.

**Q:** What do frogs eat in France?

**A:** French flies.

**Q:** What do frogs put on their bread?
**A:** Butterflies.

**Q:** What do frogs eat when they want
a hot meal?
**A:** Fireflies.

**Q:** What do frogs eat when
they're really hungry?
**A:** Horseflies.

**Q:** What do snakes eat for dessert?
**A:** Toad a la mode.

**Q:** Why did the baker put a frog in his batter?

**A:** Because he wanted to make hop cross buns.

**Q:** What do frogs eat when they go to the movies?

**A:** Croaker Jacks.

**Q:** Where do frogs put their coats when they go to the theatre?

**A:** In the croakroom.

**Q:** Why do frogs always look nervous?

**A:** Because they have butterflies in their stomachs.

**Q:** Where do frogs like to go on Saturday evenings?

**A:** The hopera.

**Q**: What's a frog's favorite ballet?
**A**: The Nutcroaker.

**Q**: Why did the frog kiss the photographer?
**A**: Because he wanted to become the handsome prints.

**Q**: How did the ugly toad reach the princess so he could kiss her?
**A**: He pulled up a toadstool.

**Q:** What do frogs hang
above their doors
on Christmas?

**A:** Mistletoad.

**Q:** What do frogs drink on Christmas?
**A:** Frognog.

**Q:** Where should you keep frognog?
**A:** In the refrogerator.

**Smart Frog:** What does a thief want to do to a bank?
**Smarter Frog:** Robbit.

**Q:** What is a bank robber's favorite kind of frog?
**A:** A safecroaker.

**Q:** What do young frogs take
to bed with them?
**A:** Toady bears.

**Q:** Why should you send a naughty frog to her room?

**A:** Because she has a bad attitoad.

**Q:** What should you do if a frog tells silly stories in his sleep?

**A:** Nothing. Let sleeping frogs lie.

**Q:** What's green and hides pots of gold at the end of rainbows?

**A:** A leaprechaun.

**Q:** What would happen if you ate a fly before going to bed?

**A:** You'd sleep like a frog.

## ABOUT THE AUTHORS

**Rick and Ann Walton** love to read, travel, play guitar, study foreign languages, and write for children. Rick also collects books and writes music while Ann knits and does origami. They live in Provo, Utah, where Ann is a computer programmer and Rick teaches frogs to tap dance. They have two phenomenal children.

## ABOUT THE ARTIST

**Susan Slattery Burke** loves to illustrate fun-loving characters, especially animals. To her, each of them has a personality all its own. Her satisfaction comes when the characters come to life for the reader as well. Susan lives in Minneapolis, Minnesota, with her husband, her daughter, and their dog and cat. A graduate of the University of Minnesota, Susan enjoys sculpting, travel, illustrating, chasing her daughter, and being outdoors.

# You Must Be Joking

**Alphabatty:** Riddles from A to Z
**Help Wanted:** Riddles about Jobs
**Here's to Ewe:** Riddles about Sheep
**Hide and Shriek:** Riddles about Ghosts and Goblins
**Ho Ho Ho!** Riddles about Santa Claus
**I Toad You So:** Riddles about Frogs and Toads
**On with the Show:** Show Me Riddles
**Out on a Limb:** Riddles about Trees and Plants
**That's for Shore:** Riddles from the Beach
**Weather or Not:** Riddles for Rain and Shine
**What's Gnu?** Riddles from the Zoo
**Wing It!** Riddles about Birds